Early Settlement in Derbyshire

Early Settlement in Derbyshire

by
P. D. Whitaker

Dalesman Books
1974

The Dalesman Publishing Company Ltd.,
Clapham (via Lancaster), Yorkshire.
First published 1974
© P. D. Whitaker, 1974

ISBN: 0 85206 228 1

Printed and bound in Great Britain by
FRETWELL & BRIAN LTD.
Silsden, Nr. Keighley, Yorkshire.

Contents

The front cover painting is by Celia King.
The title page sketch depicts an Acheulian hand-axe of the type found in the gravels at Hopton.

Preface

THE present-day Derbyshire landscape is an amalgam of natural and human processes that have been in operation for considerably varying lengths of time. This book serves as a general introduction to the processes that were to determine the character of the countryside in the time between man's arrival in Derbyshire and the arrival of the Normans. The emphasis is placed on the interplay between the early settlers and the natural environment.

Any work of this type owes much to the work of others. Generations of Derbyshire archaeologists have toiled through the best and worst of the English summers to uncover the evidence that this book draws upon. To them I can only offer my thanks. My own basis in this field was provided by time spent as a research student in the Department of Geography, University of Sheffield. I must thank my supervisor, Mr. I. S. Maxwell, for his criticisms and encouragement and Professors Waters and Gregory for their research facilities.

May I stress that many of the sites mentioned in the text are on private land. Most landowners will be pleased to grant permission to visit these sites, but ask beforehand and not when the farmer catches you in the middle of one of his fields. Keep to the footpaths where possible and shut the gates!

I.   *The Evolving Landscape*

THE county of Derbyshire is situated astride the long recognised boundary separating Highland from Lowland Britain. Consequently, a marked contrast exists between the north-western uplands, which are part of the Southern Pennines, and the south-eastern lowlands, which are part of the Trent Valley. Included within the county's limits is the greater part of the Peak District National Park, an amenity area of outstanding scenery, much used for fieldwork by students of botany, geology, archaeology and geography.

The limestone rocks deposited 280 million years ago, the gritstone "edges" exposed in the Ice Age, the Anglian villages established in the pre-Norman period, the industrialised suburbs of nineteenth century Derby and the housing estates still at the construction stage combine to form the Derbyshire scenery of today. However, this landscape has been and is a constantly changing scene. It is the outcome of long-term natural erosion and relatively short-term human interference.

This book examines the early settlement in Derbyshire in the period after man had become an influence in the modification of the countryside; this human influence was, at first, extremely limited but by the time that the Normans arrived it was established as the dominant factor in transforming the landscape. What were these influences and how did they modify the landscape of Derbyshire? These questions are answered at length in the remainder of this book; but before any changes can be measured it is necessary to know what existed before man interfered. This may be called the "natural" state.

Human interference, before the introduction of farming in the Neolithic Period, was only slight, probably limited to the accidental burning of areas of the forest. Hence for practical purposes, the landscape as it was at the opening of the Neolithic Period may be considered as being in a "natural" state. It is convenient to discuss the characteristics of the landscape in terms of the different geological formations found in Derbyshire.

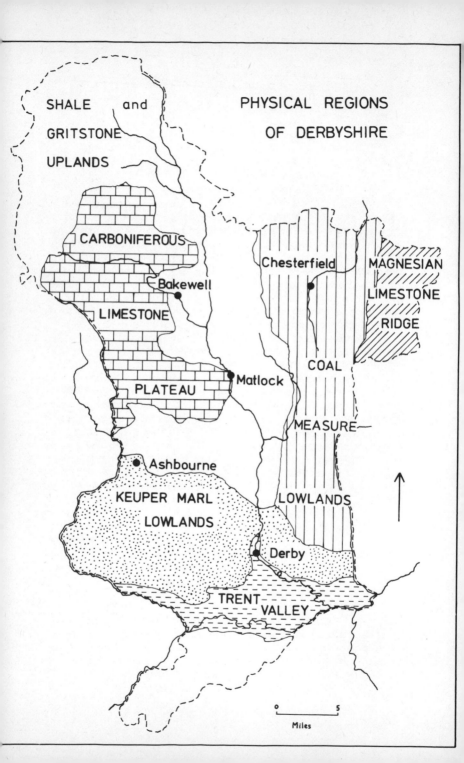

PHYSICAL REGIONS OF DERBYSHIRE

SHALE and GRITSTONE UPLANDS

CARBONIFEROUS LIMESTONE PLATEAU

Bakewell

Matlock

Ashbourne

KEUPER MARL LOWLANDS

Chesterfield

MAGNESIAN LIMESTONE RIDGE

COAL MEASURE LOWLANDS

Derby

TRENT VALLEY

0   5
Miles

The Limestone Plateau

The Carboniferous Limestone plateau occupies much of north-western Derbyshire. It is a very popular area with the visitors to the National Park. Today, the plateau surface presents a smooth, well-rounded form into which many beautiful dales incise; along some of these nature trails have been established.

Small, green fields surrounded by intricate dry-stone, limestone walls cover the area, giving an open landscape, with long-range views interrupted only where outlying hills stand up above the general plateau level. Today's openness stands in complete contrast to the woodland cover that is the natural vegetation of this area. Like a palimset, it is possible to see through this superficial modern landscape and read the partially erased evidence of former conditions beneath. On the slopes of many of the present dales can be found a woodland dominated by ash (*Fraxinus excelsior*) and with a well-developed shrub layer in which hazel (*Corylus avellana*) is the most abundant species. This is "relic" woodland for there can be little doubt that the area, at the start of the Neolithic period, was well-wooded, and that its now almost treeless nature is due to human agricultural interference.

Beneath the vegetation cover lies the all-important soil layer. Long before the use of fertilizers had become standard farming practice the inherent fertility of soils was of paramount importance to the early agriculturalists. The soils on the limestone uplands, derived not as would be expected from the underlying calcareous bedrock but from a drift of loessic material, are believed to have been very fertile under natural conditions. They were also freely-drained and almost stone free. These soil conditions combined to make the uplands an extremely attractive area to the first farmers.

The Shale and Gritstone Uplands

The Limestone plateau is almost encircled by a horseshoe shaped stretch of country, formed from grit, sandstone and shale rocks; only along the southern margin of the limestone uplands is the outcrop of this formation absent.

This upland region, with its heather (*Calluna vulgaris*) and bracken (*Pteridium aquilinum*) moorlands and peat covered surfaces, is now used mainly for the grazing of sheep, the shooting of grouse and many recreational pursuits. On the uplands settlements are scattered, being limited to isolated farmsteads, the numbers of which have been decreasing in the

last century with the decline of hill-farming. In the valleys of
the Derwent, Noe and Goyt small villages were found at the
end of the nineteenth century; now many have rapidly expanded to serve as commuter suburbs for Sheffield, Chesterfield and
Manchester. Others, such as Castleton, have adapted to meet
the needs of an increasing tourist activity. Walkers, climbers
and cyclists can be seen on practically every day of the year
trudging to the start of the *Pennine Way* at Edale, grappling
with the foot-holes on Froggatt Edge or cruising down one of the
winding enclosure lanes preserving breath for the next uphill
struggle.

As one stands on the gritstone blocks at the "Surprise
View" above Hathersage, it is quickly apparent that although
this countryside has been termed the *Dark Peak* it does not
consist of only a single landscape unit. Marked internal contrasts exist. To the south stretch the moorlands and "edges"
which characterise the uplands east of the Derwent and which
are paralleled by the similar landforms found along the western
margin of the limestone upland. In the valley below, the river
Derwent flows through the fields that were cleared from the
forests in antiquity. On a clear day, in the distance beyond Win
Hill and Mam Tor, may be discerned the high-level plateau
summit of Kinderscout, with its dissected peat surface as inhospitable now to man as at any time in the past. Just as these
contrasts can be seen today so they were found in the prehistoric period. In terms of appearance, the physical contrasts
of the landscape were not as marked as at the present day, but
without modern farming methods and good transport early
man probably regarded them as being decisive in terms of food
production and even general survival.

Turning the clock back 6,000 years, one must envisage the
alternating "edges" and scarps of these moorlands as being
covered by mixed oak forest, very similar to that which has
survived in Nether Padley Woods. The oak (*Quercus petraea*)
dominated the tree layer but birch (*Betula spp*), rowan (*Sorbus
aucuparia*) and holly (*Ilex opaca*) were all present with alder
(*Alnus glutinosa*) growing along the stream-banks and on the
poorly drained shale soils. Oak is a tree which does not cast
deep shade and this gives rise to a rich shrub and field layer with
brácken dominant. The innately infertile soils of today are
only the poor remnants of more fertile predecessors, which
were deep enough to cover the sandstone blocks that litter the
present surface. Soils varied greatly but generally over the
gritstone rocks they were sandy and freely drained and over
the shale rocks the soils had a high clay content. Consequently,

The woods at Nether Padley are one of the few places where the "natural" mixed oak forest of the gritstone moorlands can still be seen.

Mam Tor, with its massive landslide exposing the Shale Grit rocks.

they were badly drained. Good natural drainage was critical for prehistoric farming and so the areas covered by these latter soils were probably avoided, except for hunting. Other areas on East Moor which had impeded drainage were the peat bogs so familiar to today's walkers. Then, as now, they were composed of *Eriophorum vaginatum* and *Sphagnum,* formed into an absorbent carpet awkward to traverse and difficult to farm. These peat bogs were shunned by man.

The high summit surfaces of Kinderscout, Bleaklow and Featherbed Moss have, since the onset of wetter conditions in the Atlantic Period, been hostile to human settlement. Formed on the thin, alternating shales and sandstones of the Shale Grit sequence, these upland plateaux have suffered the high precipitation and widespread bad drainage necessary for the onset and continued growth of enormous areas of peat. Dissection and rapid erosion of this peat is now occurring over much of these plateaux. The cause of the degeneration is still being debated but it is likely that, in one context or another, man is to blame. Once the peat started to accumulate any serious settlement of the area was out of the question because of prehistoric man's inability to drain the land.

This lack of an adequate drainage technology probably also limited man's early attempts to settle the upper Derwent valley. Although we know little about the natural conditions of the valley in the Neolithic period, archaeologists and geographers consider it to have had a poorly drained environment. Even as late as Daniel Defoe's visit to Derbyshire (*circa* 1705), the river Derwent was susceptible to flooding in these upper stretches. There seems no reason to believe that the Neolithic Derwent valley should have been any better drained than in the eighteenth century. However, the heavy clay soils that limited pre-Saxon settlement in the English Midlands are not found in the Derwent valley proper, and thus it was only when other parts of Derbyshire were easier to settle that the valley was uninhabited. A vegetation cover of mixed oak forest would be found in the valley, but there would be an absence of birch and holly trees and an increasing dominance of alder towards the water-courses. The river itself was fully navigable to the small-draughted Neolithic canoes.

The Coal Measure Lowlands

To the east and south of the gritstone uplands is the lower ground of the Coal Measures. The physical characteristics of this region were largely determined by the alternation of shales and sandstones throughout this coal-bearing sequence. Sand-

The flatness of the river terraces is clearly seen at Borrowash.

stones from this formation never attain the dominance of their Millstone Grit counterparts, though locally they are important, as at Ambergate.

The alternating rocks dip strongly eastwards resulting in a distinct north-south grain to the landscape. Long ridges of sandstone form the high ground with shale-floored valleys between. Where the sandstones are dominant a sandy soil formed, supporting a covering of mixed oak forest, but shale is the bedrock that underlies much of the area. On this latter formation fine-textured, poorly drained soils would have arisen, with a dense covering of woodland inhospitable to early settlers.

The Keuper Marl Lowlands

Stretching in a broad band across the south of the county are the rocks that belong to the Triassic system. This is made up of many types of sandstones, pebble beds, shales and marls but only two need be considered here—the Bunter Sandstone and the Keuper Marls.

The Bunter Sandstones crop out in the Mercaston area, but it is further to the east in the Sherwood Forest region of Nottinghamshire that the formation is widely exposed. Although capable of supporting a "primitive" form of woodland characterised by an extreme paucity of species, these sandy soils are regarded as being sterile from the farming point of view. This is one reason why Sherwood Forest has survived into the modern era.

The Keuper Marls have given rise to the low-lying country from Derby southwards to the Trent. These lowlands are however far from flat—rather they form a moderately dissected hilly region. Soils derived from the Keuper Marls had a clayey-loam texture with imperfect drainage. The woodland would have been of the mixed oak type but with plenty of water-loving alder present. Early man appears to have had considerable difficulty in adapting his agricultural technology to master these heavy soils.

The Magnesian Limestone Ridge

Forming the eastern boundary of the county is a narrow plateau, up to five miles wide, of Magnesian Limestone. In places this ridge is transversed by sharply cut watergaps, in one of which is situated the famous Creswell Caves, discussed in the next chapter. The soils found over the limestone are, unlike those on the Carboniferous Limestone uplands, derived from the rock. They are freely drained, partially leached sandy clays containing nodules of yellow weathering Magnesian Limestone. As with the other limestone region, Neolithic man is likely to have found the Magnesian Limestone ridge covered by ash and hazel woods.

The Trent Valley

As the name implies this region covers the Derbyshire stretch of the Trent valley, but in addition to this area the lower Derwent valley and the Dove valley, east of Uttoxeter, must be considered as part of the same formation. Along the banks of these three rivers successive changes in the water level have left marked terrace features. These terraces are important but the modern floodplain dominates the landscape. All these features were present in the Neolithic period.

The rocks of the river terraces give rise to a variety of soils, sandy and clayey soils, loams and intermediate forms being known. Mixed oak forest and easy-to-work soils enabled pre-historic man to make early use of the terraces. The floodplain must have had poorly drained soils susceptible to seasonal floodings. Alder would have been associated with this water-logged habitat. Through this area flowed the river Trent, which gave invaders from the east coast access into the heart of Derbyshire.

This rather academic view of Neolithic conditions is a nec-essary prologue to the understanding of the changes in the landscape that were to follow the arrival of man. These changes were a long way off; before man could alter the countryside he passed through nearly a million years when he was at the mercy of Nature.

2.   *Hunters and Gatherers*

M AN first arrived in Derbyshire approximately 800,000 years ago during the Ice Age. More correctly this should be termed the Pleistocene period. It was essentially an era in the Earth's history, starting about three million years ago, during which the area of our planet covered by ice drastically increased. At their maximum extent, ice-sheets covered almost one-third of the Earth's land surface, compared with the one-tenth that they occupy today. The "Ice Age" was a series of at least four main glaciations moving across the Northern Hemisphere and then retreating back to the Arctic Basin. The glaciations were separated from each other by warm intervals, termed interglacial periods. It is not yet clear whether the "Ice Age" has really ended, for today we may be living in such an interglacial period and in time ice-sheets may once again advance over Europe. For convenience the period since the retreat of the last ice-sheet from Britain is called the post-glacial. This started about 13,000 years ago.

During a glacial period there was a vast amount of water held on the land in the form of ice. As there is only a finite quantity of water upon Earth this resulted in a world-wide lowering of sea-level. Britain had a vastly different shape to that of today and was still linked to the Continent of Europe by a wide land-bridge. In an interglacial period the ice-caps retreated, releasing their water back into the oceans with a consequent rise in sea-level. This reduced the land area of Britain as well as diminishing the width of the land-bridge. However, it was not until the post-glacial period that Britain actually became separated from the Continent about 6000B.C.

The environmental conditions discussed in chapter one did not influence settlement until the Neolithic farmers started to cultivate the land. In the early history of man's settlement of Derbyshire only three major environments need to be considered—glacial, periglacial and interglacial. During the Mendel and Riss glaciations, ice-sheets covered the whole of Derbyshire and climatic conditions were too harsh for man to settle the area. In the periods before and immediately after the

19

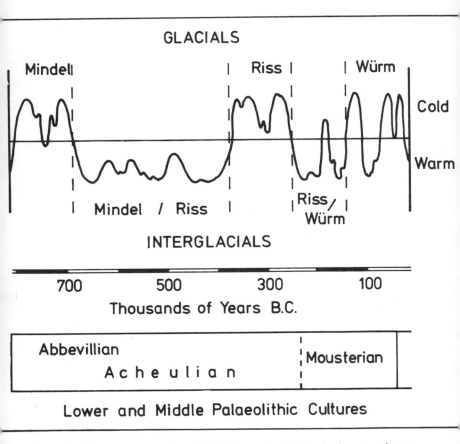

GLACIALS

Mindel

Riss

Würm

Cold

Warm

Mindel / Riss

Riss/
Würm

INTERGLACIALS

700   500   300   100

Thousands of Years B.C.

Abbevillian
A c h e u l i a n

Mousterian

Lower and Middle Palaeolithic Cultures

The Pleistocene succession in Britain correlated with the human cultures of Derbyshire.

glaciations, Derbyshire experienced sub-Arctic or periglacial conditions. Under these the climate was very cold in winter but mild in summer. As in the present-day Arctic the tundra was able to support a sparse covering of vegetation sufficient to allow herds of reindeer, wild horse and mammoths to graze. Man was also able to live in this climate and he survived by hunting the herds of migrating animals.

In complete contrast to these environments stands that of the interglacial periods. These experienced climatic conditions similar and often better than today with forests and grasslands spreading back over the land. The fauna of the tundra gave way

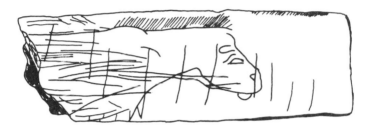

An Upper Palaeolithic carving of a horse's head, engraved on a fragment of bone. From Creswell Caves. (Plaster cast in Sheffield Museum).

to a forest fauna of deer, wild pig, wild cattle, bear and hyena. Man was able to support himself from this rich source of animals, which provided him with meat, skins and bones; he supplemented his diet by fishing and gathering wild berries and nuts, which were plentiful.

The earliest record of man living in Derbyshire comes from the high-level glacial deposits and river terraces along the banks of the Trent. These deposits were laid down after the Wurm or last glaciation but are made up of material which was weathered from the rocks of the Derbyshire uplands in the Mindel to Wurm period, a total span of about 700,000 years. Only the non-perishable artifacts of these lower Palaeolithic, or Old Stone Age, people have survived in the unstratified gravels, especially at Hilton. These artifacts enable archaeologists to recognise cultural groupings. The hand-axes of the culture associated with the earliest man in Britain—the Abbevillians—have been found at Hilton. These people were followed into the area by Acheulian men who roamed and

21

hunted in Derbyshire during the Mindel/Riss and Riss/Wurm interglacials. No complete record of Acheulian man can be found for erosion has stripped the Derbyshire landscape of the soils over which he hunted. A flint hand-axe used by these people was found in high-level gravels at Hopton. From this find and others throughout Britain and Europe it is clear that the Acheulians were nomadic hunters and gatherers wandering over large tracts of land in small bands. The famous Swanscombe skull, which is thought by some anthropologists to be an early form of *Homo Sapiens,* is associated with implements of Acheulian tradition.

The Middle Palaeolithic period is represented by finds of the Mousterian culture, which was associated with Neanderthal man (*Homo Neanderthalensis*). Neat and finely worked flint core tools are characteristic of this period. These people arrived in the Midlands in the Riss/Wurm interglacial and stayed until the last interstadial of the Wurm glaciation.

This Palaeolithic sequence is best represented in the renowned Creswell Caves. The site at Creswell Crags, on the Magnesian Limestone ridge, has long been known as one of immense importance to British prehistory. The limestone at Creswell has been eroded to give a series of caves in which a complete cultural sequence from the Middle Palaeolithic to the Mesolithic period has been preserved. Not only is evidence of human occupation abundant but bones of animals, together with indications of climatic change, have been recorded.

When the Neanderthal hunters first took up residence in the Pinhole Cave the Wurm ice-sheets had not yet advanced across Europe. The hunters lived on a land with forest and steppe conditions and hunted horse, bison, woolly rhinoceros and mammoth. In their shelters they lit fires to keep away the cave-bears, hyenas and cave-lions. The Wurm glaciation began and the deteriorating climate gradually brought tundra and sub-Arctic conditions to Derbyshire, forcing Neanderthal man and the larger mammals to migrate southwards to warmer climates. A partial retreat of the ice enabled man to reoccupy the Pinhole Cave before a further ice advance once more forced him out of the area. When the warmer climates next prevailed, in an interstadial period, the Mousterians came back to Creswell but their stay was shortened by the arrival of *Homo Sapiens* with their Upper Palaeolithic blade culture.

The Upper Palaeolithic period can be divided into cultures using a tool-form known as a "backed-blade" (i.e. the blade has one of its edges blunted for holding or hafting) and those not using this technique. The Aurignacian culture is one that

The caves at Creswell Crags. They were excavated from 1875 onwards by the Rev. Magins Mello and Professor Boyd Dawkins. A. L. Armstrong did further work in the caves for the British Association between 1922 and 1935, and a modern excavation was undertaken by J. B. Cambell when quarrying threatened to destroy some of the sites.

A Mesolithic encampment. Stag's horns were worn by the men when they went hunting.

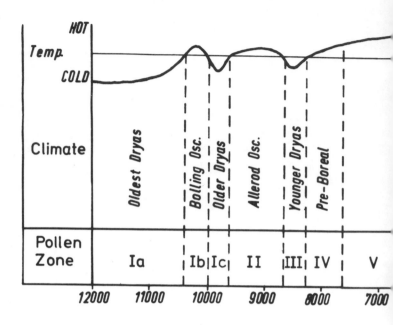

Culture: CRESWELLIAN

does not use backed-blading, and people of this culture appear to have been the first *Homo Sapiens* in the area. They were replaced by the Gravettians, who were "backed-bladers". After ice had once again advanced and retreated over Northern Britain the climate grew milder, the woolly rhinoceros and mammoth died out and eventually even the reindeer disappeared.

This climatic improvement is part of the Late Glacial period and by Allerod times the hunters were relying on deer and wild cattle for much of their food. With the change in diet came a change in the tools required to kill and prepare the new food. The cultural traits which resulted bridged the gap between the full Upper Palaeolithic and the full Mesolithic periods. One

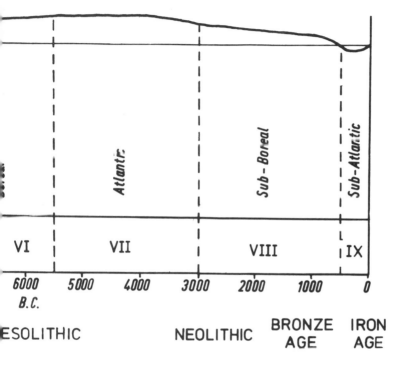

The Postglacial climatic succession in Derbyshire and its associated human cultures.

of the cultures that forms this bridge in Britain is the Creswell, named from its Derbyshire type-site. It is characterised by small flint tools, with Gravettian origins, including backed-blades, obliquely blunted blades and shouldered points. The culture reached its pinnacle in the Allerod period, which in Derbyshire has been dated to 9640 B.C. Finds of this culture are not only found on the Magnesian Limestone ridge but also are known from the Dowel, Elder Bush and Thor Fissure caves on the Carboniferous Limestone plateau.

This "epi-palaeolithic" culture gave way to Mesolithic cultures in the post-glacial period. The story of the post-glacial climatic changes has been revealed by various techniques, of which one of the most fruitful has been the recognition and interpretation of pollen grains that survive in some types of deposits. From a study of these "fossil" pollen grains, botanists have been able to show that the early part of the post-glacial period is characterised by a warming of the climate. This warming manifested itself in the landscape by a growth in the forests during the Boreal period. About 5500 B.C. the rainfall increased and in Derbyshire the deposition of the peat, which now covers the Kinderscout and Bleaklow plateaux, was initiated. These areas have remained treeless since this date.

The Creswell culture appears to have lasted until well into the seventh millenium B.C. before being superseded by the French Sauveterrian culture, which had spread to Britain certainly before the end of the Boreal period. The Sauveterrians had strongly microlithic tendencies, with marked geometric tool forms including tiny crescents and triangular shapes. They had little use for axes. This is surprising for the growth of forests led other Mesolithic cultures, such as the Maglemosian, to develop the true axe to meet the need for a tree-felling and woodworking tool. A few implements in the Maglemosian tradition are known from the high hills of the Pennines but it is the Sauveterrian culture which dominates the Mesolithic period of Derbyshire.

It has often been said that Mesolithic man had a preference for sandy soils but this is a fallacy. The Coal Measure shales of Derbyshire have yielded flint implements belonging to this period. The explanation behind this fallacy is that the artifacts are most noticeable upon sandy sites whereas upon clay they are not easily detected. Sites of the Sauveterrian culture are known from the Pennines where wind action has eroded the peat to expose the underlying mineral soil. Here, worked flints are often associated with hearths which are all that is left of temporary camps where the hunters sat around a fire, making a new set of arrows or barbs. Elsewhere on the grit-stone moorlands natural erosion has stripped much of the area of the soil of that period and Mesolithic finds are rarer. Similarly, Mesolithic material is scarce from the Carboniferous Limestone uplands, except in the caves mentioned previously. This must reflect the easily erodable nature of its surface for Mesolithic man is known to have used the chert rocks from the limestone sequence in the Wye Valley to make his tools in preference to or when supplies of flint were limited.

The Sauveterrians had a hunting and food-gathering economy, hunting deer, wild cattle and wild pig and gathering hazel nuts. The general distribution of their artifacts suggests that these people lived and hunted in the upper zone of open woodland between 1,200 and 1,600 feet, but this may be due to the non-preservation of material from other environments.

In the caves at Creswell, and in other Magnesian Limestone caves, finds from this period have been recorded. One cave, Whaley No. 2, contained a female Mesolithic skull, one of the few places in Britain where Mesolithic skeletal material has been found.

The Derbyshire landscape was beginning to take on some of its characteristic features of today. On the high plateaux of Kinderscout, Bleaklow and Featherbed Moss the blanket bogs of peat were being deposited. Soils were starting to mature under the cover of primeval woodland, which clothed much of Derbyshire. Man had not yet learned to control the growth of the forests. It was the Neolithic, or New Stone Age, people who developed and applied the technique of forest clearance. They arrived in Britain about 3500 B.C., but it was not until at least five hundred years later that they began to settle parts of Derbyshire, and even then it is likely that Mesolithic peoples remained in the area for a considerable time before they were absorbed into later cultures.

3.   *The First Farmers*

D URING the Palaeolithic and Mesolithic periods men lived by hunting, fishing and gathering wild plants. This food-gathering economy was gradually replaced by a food-producing economy which marks the start of the Neolithic period. The change laid the foundations for civilisation to develop. Hitherto, man had been dependent on the number of animals and wild plants that the natural conditions could support. When game animals moved on their seasonal migrations, man was forced to follow. His life had to be nomadic if he was to survive. The adoption of crop production and the domestication of animals meant that he was able to settle in one place, to band together in larger groups for commercial production of food and defence against enemies and eventually to provide enough surplus food to support specialised craftsmen, who could manufacture tools and pottery.

The word *"Neolithic"* although originally meaning the "New Stone Age", now implies a cultural stage in which food production based on crops and domesticated animals, without the use of metals, is practised. It was in the Near East that the *Neolithic Revolution* is thought to have begun, about 10,000 B.C., but it was not until *circa* 3000 B.C. that the first farmers arrived in Britain from the Continent. The first settlers came from northern France, Germany and the Low Countries. In Britain their culture is called *Windmill Hill* after one of their camp sites found in Wiltshire. The chalklands of England must have proved suitable for their farming systems as sites associated with these people are found along the chalk ridges of Wessex, as well as on the Cretaceous Chalk of Lincolnshire and Yorkshire.

The Windmill Hill people wore skins and textiles, used flint tools and stone axes and introduced pottery into this country. Their dead were buried in earthen long barrows, which contained collective inhumation burials, although some of the Yorkshire examples contain cremations. In Derbyshire these long barrows are entirely absent, as is the pottery of these early people. The conclusion drawn is that inland penetration

30

Neolithic bowl and arrowhead from Church Dale.

Sketch of Five Wells Neolithic chambered tomb, Taddington.

by these people did not reach our area, which must still have been settled by the Mesolithic hunters.

The aboriginal Mesolithic population of Britain did not disappear overnight. Rather they continued their life much as before and only gradually assimilated the elements of the Neolithic economy. We find them attempting to make crude pottery, imitating the habits and finally interbreeding with the newcomers. The resultant cultures have been termed the Secondary Neolithic. Various regional groupings are recognised, although only one need concern the student of Derbyshire's prehistory—the Peterborough. This amalgam of several round-bottomed, decorated pottery types is associated with fish-spears and other hunting equipment which indicates that these people still practised some parts of the traditional life style even though they had now become farmers. The long barrows of the Windmill Hill people were superseded by the construction of round, megalithic tombs.

Neolithic Derbyshire was an area in which the new culture was *absorbed* rather than *imposed*. The basic elements of the population were Mesolithic descendants who could trace their origins back to the Creswellian period. Into this group were grafted Neolithic folk. This new group arrived sometime about the middle of the third millenium B.C.; where they came from is uncertain but it has been claimed that entry into Derbyshire was from a south-western direction. The claim is based upon the fact that a megalithic tomb, known as the Bridestones, near Congleton, is earlier than any of the tombs in Derbyshire.

Associated with the spread of the Neolithic Revolution, but not directly linked to it, is the practice of building megalithic monuments. Mention has already been made of the long barrows built by the Windmill Hill people, but in the Peak the first tombs were constructed much later and have a circular form. There are seven chambered tombs in Derbyshire but the Bridestones in Cheshire and Long Low in Staffordshire are all part of the same complex of remains. These tombs, which are usually in the form of a passage grave leading off a simple forecourt, enclosed in a circular mound, have been all but destroyed by erosion and excavations, both authorised and unauthorised. Excavations have shown the tombs to contain inhumated bodies, at least eighteen at Ringham Low, but to be very poor in grave goods.

Chambered tombs were not the only form of burying the dead. In 1938 Major Harris discovered two disarticulated skeletons in a cist-like structure which used the natural rock wall as one of its sides. The skeletons were accompanied by

A reconstruction of the type of cattle, Bos primigenius, domesticated by Neolithic farmers in Derbyshire.

sherds of Peterborough pottery, a *petit-tranchit* derivative arrow-head and some flint flakes.

The Neolithic tombs are limited to the Carboniferous Limestone plateau south of the river Wye. Manby was the first person to see that these chambered tombs could be divided into two separate groups—a northern group consisting of Five Wells, Bole Hill and Ringham Low and a southern group consisting of Green Low, Minninglow, Stoney Low and Harborough. The little that is known about the actual settlement areas of this period fits in with this distribution. To the northern group can be linked the Peterborough ware found in Calling Low Dale, the Neolithic artifacts from Horsborough and the Neolithic-type flint implements discovered on the pre-barrow surface under the Bronze Age barrow at Haddon Grove Farm. An implied settlement on or near Elton Common, located by Radley and Cooper, is situated among the tombs of the southern group and the local area has yielded assemblages of Neolithic flaked flints.

The only known Neolithic settlement within Derbyshire is on the river terraces at Aston-upon-Trent. Under a later barrow were sealed a hearth, pits and a carbonized grain of emmer (wheat), which had a radiocarbon date of 2800 B.C., placing them well within the Neolithic period. However, sherds of undecorated pottery from this site seem to be derived from the Windmill Hill culture, and this may be older than the tombs just considered.

The very nature of the surviving remains means that we know more about the dead of this period than about the living, working population. These people must have been farmers but the Derbyshire record of this occupation is limited to the grains of emmer found at Aston. From evidence recovered elsewhere in Britain it is possible to infer the farming techniques used.

The land was still well-wooded and the animals which were domesticated were those that were primarily forest creatures. Domesticated cattle were descended from the wild aurochs (*Bos primigenius*). These descendants had smaller bodies than the wild form but were nevertheless considerably larger than modern cattle. Domesticated *Bos primigenius* are known from British sites but not from Derbyshire sites. Bones found in the excavation of Green Low chambered tomb belonged to short-horned cattle, the so-called *Bos longifrons*, at one time thought not to have appeared in Britain until later Bronze Age times. This animal was almost a dwarf version of the *Bos primigenius* and is considered to have evolved as a result of a near starvation diet in the process of domestication. Wild pig, *Sus scrofa*, was common in the forests and its bones have been found on numerous sites. Sheep or goat, *Ovis* or *Capra*, are not easy to distinguish when found as archaeological remains but it would appear that in Derbyshire these animals were not farmed until clearances within the forests had made open pasture available.

On the limestone uplands small areas of the forest would be cleared, not only for pasture—this would probably have been a secondary development—but also for the growing of crops. The limited evidence available suggests that wheat was the most common grain grown, with patches of barley also being farmed. It is a common assumption among prehistorians that the British Neolithic farmers did not possess a plough and that the soil was turned by the use of a light wooden hoe. However, traces of cross-ploughing have been recognised elsewhere in Britain beneath Bronze Age barrows. Whether these traces are dated to the Neolithic or the very beginning of the Bronze Age is still not certain.

Before the grain could be sown the forest had to be cleared. To help him Neolithic man evolved the finely-polished stone axes, which were more efficient than their Mesolithic predecessors. Many varieties of suitable rocks were used, and great trouble was taken to set up trade routes to ensure that the specialised axe-producing craftsmen could distribute their wares.

As in the past flint was in great demand, much of it being supplied by the mines of Grimes Graves in Norfolk. However, the near monopoly of flint was now challenged by the tougher, igneous rocks found throughout Highland Britain. Microscopical examination of the axe heads has enabled geologists to locate the sites of many of the early axe factories. Many stone tools of this period are known from Derbyshire. The Neolithic folk of this county seem to have established trading links with the craftsmen of the Lake District, North and South Wales, Shropshire and Cornwall, and in at least one case with Antrim in Ireland. Although the process of producing these axes is reasonably simple, it must have involved hours of intricate workmanship. After a suitably sized piece of rock had been broken from the quarry face the axe head was shaped by flaking. This was followed by grinding down the surface on a wetted stone slab until a fine polish had been achieved all over the implement. The axe head was then hafted into a wooden handle.

With this improved tool man began to make inroads into

the forest. Clearings were made by the "slash and burn" method, i.e. cutting down and burning the trees. The soil and resulting ash were raked with either a light plough or a hoe to incorporate the seeds. When ripe the cereals were harvested with a stone scythe. The quantity of cereals produced was not great for we know by the large number of bones from young animals found on some sites that these had to be slaughtered in the autumn. There was only sufficient food to feed the family and a few breeding stock throughout the winter.

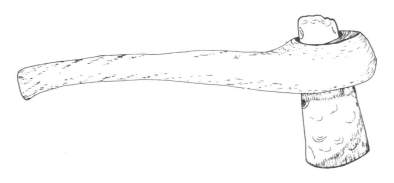

A Neolithic stone axe, hafted in a wooden handle.

Little has been said of the living accommodation of these farmers. Timber settlements in the clearances must have been the rule but the caves of the area offered ready-made shelter to many Neolithic families. We can only suggest inspired ideas as to how these people lived but about 1700 Daniel Defoe, while undertaking *A Tour Through the Whole Island of Great Britain*, met a family of seven who lived in a cave upon Brassington Moor, Derbyshire. His description of the cave and its occupants, with minor modifications, sets one's imagination wandering back to the third millenium B.C.:

> "There was a large hollow cave, which the poor people by two curtains hanged across, had parted into three rooms On one side was a chimney, . . . through the rock to carry the smoke out at the top . . . Every thing was clean and neat, though mean and ordinary. There were shelves with

earthenware, . . . There was, which I observed in particular, a whole flitch or side of bacon hanging up in the chimney, and by it a good piece of another. There was a sow and pigs running about at the door, and a little lean cow feeding upon a green place just before the door, and a little enclosed piece of ground I mentioned (*near the mouth of the cave*) was growing with good barley; it being then near harvest."

The head of the household in this case was a lead miner, but in the Neolithic period he would have been occupied maintaining a larger herd of cattle and pigs and cultivating a larger field of barley if this family was to survive the winter months.

Of the political and social units of life we know little, but we can suggest that at certain times of the year large numbers of people gathered together, first of all in causewayed camps (absent from Derbyshire) and later in henges. The henge was a circular monument, with a central area surrounded by a ditch and bank, unique to the British Isles. Their purpose is far from clear. Early archaeologists thought that they must have been used for religious ceremonies, but more informed recent opinion has it that they may have been sites of social gatherings, similar to the seasonal fairs in the Middle Ages.

Derbyshire can lay claim to four of these important monuments. The best known, Arbor Low, the "Stonehenge of the North", is found on the limestone uplands near Monyash. It is matched by the similarly sized but less known henge near Chapel-en-le-Frith, known locally as the "Bull Ring". These two were the last of the four henges to be constructed. They were preceded by two almost completely forgotten henges—Standen Low, south of Buxton, which is now much eroded, and an even earlier henge next to Arbor Low. This proto-Arbor Low has no surface manifestations and is only visible on aerial photographs.

The Beaker Folk

About the time that Arbor Low was being built, Britain was invaded by peoples from the Low Countries. The East Coast was the first area to feel the influences of these migrants. The Beaker folk, as these people have become known, are represented by a culture that is transitional between the "Stone Age" and the full Bronze Age. The main feature of this culture is the practice of burying a "beaker" with the dead, presumably to hold a drink for the dead person's journey to the next world.

The Beaker folk had a slightly different physical appearance

The "henge" monument of Arbor Low, near Monyash. Its scale can be judged from the animals on the bank which are cattle.

A Beaker group from Green Low, Alsop Moor.

to the aboriginal population of Britain; they were round-headed in contrast to the long-headed Neolithic people. Besides this physical difference, the two cultures varied in that the Beaker folk had knowledge of the manufacturing process involved in producing metal tools. Metallurgy was in its infancy; initially only copper tools were brought to the British Isles by these immigrants. It is possible that the main motive behind the "invasion" by these peoples was to open new markets for their goods as well as to prospect for new copper sources.

Advancing along the Trent and Don valleys, a small number of Beaker migrants entered Derbyshire from east Yorkshire and settled with the Neolithic peoples upon the limestone plateau. The finding of a beaker in the Neolithic Green Low chambered tomb suggests that in time a certain amount of the Beaker folk's culture was absorbed by the aboriginal inhabitants (or vice versa). Once initial contact had been established a much larger wave of Beaker folk moved northwards from Wessex and the Fens. The arrival of these folk caused a movement of the Neolithic peoples on to the gritstone moorlands.

The timber settlements of this period have long since disappeared and our knowledge is more about the dead than the living. The dead were greatly revered for considerable trouble was taken in their burial. Interments were usually in a neatly-formed cist. The corpse was buried with its knees folded up to its chest—as in the mother's womb—and was accompanied by a profusion of elegantly-shaped instruments of flint and bone, together with the traditional highly-decorated beaker. Over the top of the stone cist were placed roughly-hewn blocks of the local limestone until the whole was formed into a round barrow. The white colour of the rock must have provided a striking contrast to the surrounding dark green vegetation. Round barrows are abundant in northern Derbyshire where past generations of countryfolk have known them as "lows", e.g. Bee Low, Blake Low, End Low and Elk Low.

One of the commonest flint implements associated with Beaker burials is the "barbed and tanged" arrowhead. Together with stone guards used by archers to protect their wrists against the return of the bow string which are sometimes found with burials, these arrowheads show that hunting must still have been an important part of the economy. However, these people were primarily stock-raisers who practised simple cultivation of barley and wheat and hunted to supplement their diet.

At Swarkeston are found four Early Bronze Age barrows.

*A re-drawing of a "Burial of the Ancient Britons" used as the frontispiece
to Thomas Bateman's "Vestiges of the Antiquities of Derbyshire" published
in 1848.*

In the process of investigating one of these burial monuments the excavator—Ernest Greenfield—found that sealed by the barrow was an occupation level dating to the Beaker period. Greenfield traced the positions of post-holes and stake-holes in the subsoil and suggested that they indicated wooden structures for human and animal use. He concluded that "the area was occupied by an agricultural community of Beaker date who were probably also sheep breeders." A similar occupation level has been found on the gravel terraces at Willington where further excavation will take place to try and unravel the complex dating involved on a site that was occupied by various cultures throughout later prehistory. These two sites, with additional information from Aston, Barrow, Stenson and Twyford, show that the Trent gravel terraces were farmed in considerable density by the Beaker folk. This is not surprising as the soils tend to be sandy, well-drained and easily worked.

In the Beaker period it has been shown that the two areas settled by these folk were the limestone uplands and the river terraces of the Trent valley. The former area is now characterised by Beaker burials, the latter area by Beaker occupation sites. Whether there was this distinction when these folk actually dwelt in Derbyshire or whether the distinction has arisen from the differences in environmental changes is an academic argument not yet resolved.

4.   *Bronze Age Metalworkers*

PEOPLE with a Neolithic culture still roamed Britain for many centuries after the first invasion of the Beaker folk. These people were influenced by the newcomers, as is clearly shown in the work of the native potters who ceased producing Peterborough Ware and replaced it with the food vessel. The latter is an amalgam of native and Beaker traditions; the hollow neck and frequent use of cord impressions are derived from Peterborough customs but the flat base and horizontal pattern are clearly drawn from Beaker pottery.

Care must be taken in interpreting evidence of this new culture. The changeover from the use of one type of pottery to another does not necessarily infer that a new group of people have migrated into the area. Thus it would be wrong to assume that the appearance of the food vessel in Derbyshire was as a result of a fresh invasion of people, and it is better to think of the inhabitants gradually absorbing a new cultural trait. The local potters seem to have tried to reach a compromise between beakers and food vessels for in a burial at Elk Low there was found a pot which can only be seen as a mixture of the two styles. It is the only one of its kind known from Derbyshire which suggests that any resistance to the new pottery was short lived. The food vessel idea arrived via the Trent valley about 1650 B.C. Its use was limited in time and it was probably not employed after about 1475 B.C.

Once again very little is known about the settlements of these food vessel users, which is not surprising if the pots were used by the Beaker folk in their timber dwellings. Information is limited to the burials of the period. Round barrows were used to store the bodies of these pottery users and inhumation was still practised, but the strict observance of a set crouched position for the corpse was no longer important. Of course, the beaker was replaced with the food vessel—so named because of its apparent function. For the first time significant metal tools are found. The slender copper/bronze awls of the beaker burials gave way to solid bronze daggers with impressive

44

BRONZE AGE POTTERY TYPES
FROM DERBYSHIRE

0   4
Cms

SHORT NECK or 'C' BEAKER
Blakelow

LONG NECK or 'A' BEAKER
Rusden Low

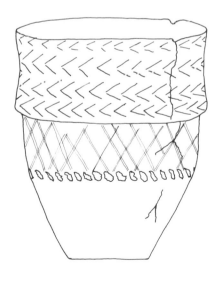

CINERARY URN
Flax Dale

FOOD VESSEL
Longstone Edge

After E. Howarth, "Catalogue of
the Bateman Collection of
Antiquities", London, 1899

PDW 1970

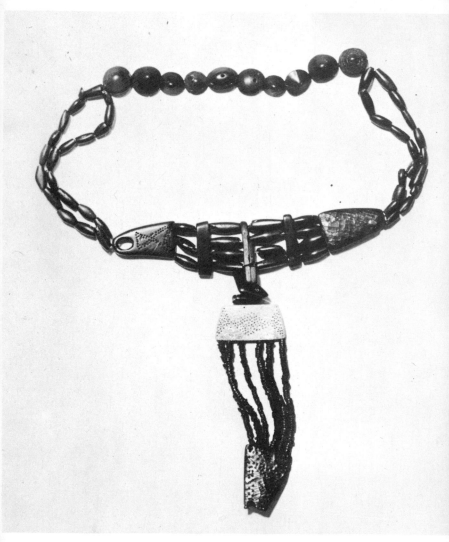

Jet necklace from barrow at Arbor Low.

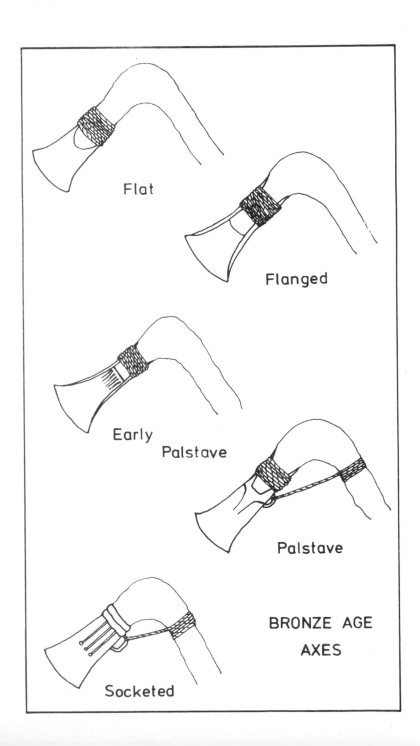

Flat

Flanged

Early Palstave

Palstave

Socketed

BRONZE AGE AXES

riveted handles.

Equally impressive are the fine jet necklaces which belong to this era. A selection of jet jewellery is on permanent display at Sheffield City Museum. Individual necklaces contain over a hundred hand-carved pieces and the complete necklace usually had three or four strands of oblong, round or disc-shaped beads held apart by decorated, flat plates. The archaeological interest in these objects stems from the limited outcrop of jet in Britain. Since prehistoric times this hard, black substance has been mined on the north-eastern coast of Yorkshire, centered on Whitby. The presence of these necklaces in Derbyshire is proof of cultural and trading links between these two areas. The importance of these trading links will be shown later.

Many barrows from this period are found on the limestone hills; the excavation of some of these being carried out by Thomas Bateman in the early nineteenth century. On 21st April, 1849, Bateman and Mr. S. Carrington excavated a barrow near Cauldon which was to prove to belong to the Food Vessel people. From his record we learn that:

> "Digging to the depth of four feet, in the centre, through earth and stones, we discovered the skeleton of a young person laid upon the ribs of an ox or other large animal placed transversly to the human bones, at regular intervals side by side. At the North side of the barrow was a rock grave, the bottom of which was about two feet beneath the turf, containing the skeleton of another young person, accompanied by a very neatly-ornamented vase (*food vessel*), five inches high, and nine instruments of white flint, . . . The vase retained its upright position, having been placed upon a flat stone, and likewise protected by another standing on edge by its side."

Bateman's methods were crude. With unskilled farm labourers, he was capable of opening four or five barrows a day—a task impossible by modern standards of excavation. Whether saint or sinner, it is almost entirely due to his efforts that there is so much information available about Derbyshire's prehistory.

Turning to the living Food Vessel people, we can see little difference between their life-style and that of the Beaker folk. They were undoubtedly small-scale farmers producing cereals and raising cattle and sheep, which were becoming more widely reared as the woodlands were slowly but necessarily cleared.

Some of these people must have made their livings as traders because besides the presence of "Whitby" jet in these peoples' barrows there are influences in the pottery which are distinctly Irish—indeed one variety of food vessel is known as an Irish Vase. It is not difficult to establish in what commodities these people were trading. The Irish people of this time have long been known as metalworkers and goldsmiths. As the number of bronze tools found in Derbyshire increases with the arrival of the food vessels it is natural to see the trading commodity as bronze. Trade routes have been recognised across the northern Pennines, via the Ribble, Aire and Calder valleys. Now it appears that a route through the Mersey and Trent valleys should be accepted, with the trade controlled by the Food Vessel people of the Peak.

Bronze axes were very expensive. Stone axes were still in use for cutting down trees, with the bronze tools being used for limited purposes and on ceremonial occasions.

The Urnfolk

Elsewhere in the British Isles, Neolithic influences could still be found. Peterborough Ware gave way to a new form of pot—the Cinerary (or Collared) Urn—which had two functions. It was used as a storage vessel by the living and as a receptacle for their cremated bones by the dead.

An expansion or migration of people using these pots brought them into Derbyshire. Bu'lock has shown that these people came from south Lancashire; on arrival they settled on what are now the high moorlands of East Moor. Past authors have suggested that this new area was colonised either because the limestone plateau was already fully occupied by the Food Vessel people or there was a decrease in the rainfall which resulted in the limestone area becoming too dry to grow crops. However, these people came from the part of Lancashire in which sandy soils are common and their farming must have been adapted to this soil. It seems reasonable to suppose that when they moved into Derbyshire they would look for land with environmental conditions similar to those they had left. These conditions were found on the present gritstone moors and not on the limestone uplands.

Anyone familiar with the moorlands of today cannot have failed to notice the many remnants left behind by these Urnfolk. From the lower levels of Kinderscout and Bleaklow plateaux, in a wide semi-circular sweep across Nether, Abney Moscar, Burbage, Big and Beeley Moors to Matlock these moorlands have suffered little damage from arable farming. In consequence we can now study the huts, fields, burials and

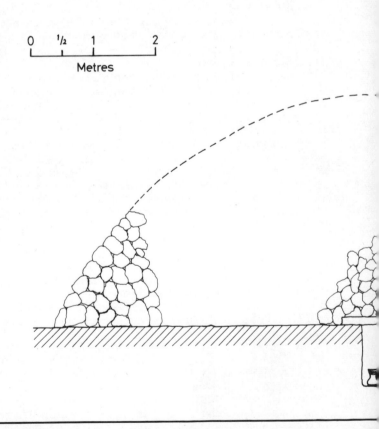

0 ½ 1 2
Metres

IN AN EARLY BRONZE AGE BARROW

1 Primary Beaker Inhumation
2 Secondary Food Vessel Cremation
3 Secondary "Urn" Cremation

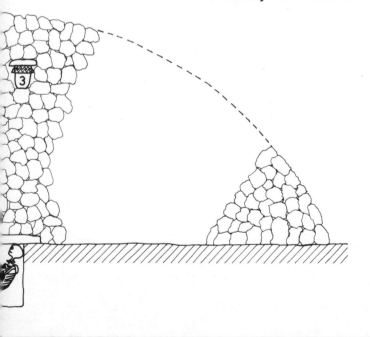

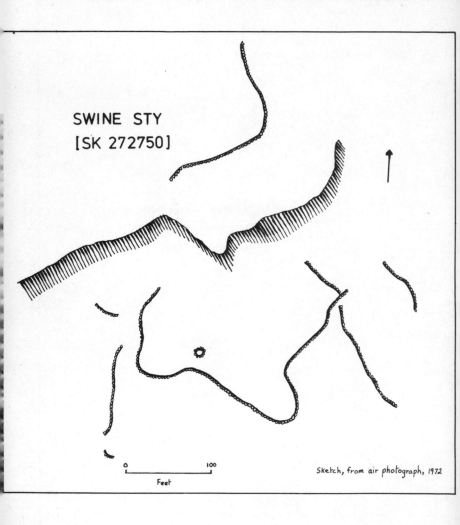

SWINE STY
[SK 272750]

0   100

Feet

Sketch, from air photograph, 1972

religious sites that were used by the Urnfolk in 1550 B.C.

Stanton Moor, near Birchover, is an isolated area of grit-stone close to the main limestone mass. The moor appears to have been popular with the Urnfolk for the surface is dotted with their barrows. Excavation of these has shown that the dead were cremated, not inhumed. At the northern end of the moor is the "Nine Ladies" stone circle made up of, as the name suggests, nine upright stones. The distribution of stone circles is comparable to that of Urnfolk burials and it seems that they were built by the same people. Ideas of their function vary. Some experts state that they were ritual sites while others see them as astronomical devices for fixing calendar dates. One of these circles, above Froggatt Edge, is still covered by heather and bracken and contrasts sharply with the clean cut appear-ance of the "Nine Ladies", which is in the care of the Depart-ment of the Environment.

Mention must be made of the numerous huts and fields known. The huts have survived because they were built mainly from local gritstone. They are not as well preserved as the Dartmoor examples but nevertheless it is not hard to imagine them as they once were, surrounded by low field walls. The circular tradition associated with the Urnfolks' constructions is strictly adhered to in the round huts, which are 10–30 feet across. With the clearings for these farms having been cut from the virgin forest it is likely that the fields would only be used for crops—animals could be allowed to wander within the forest.

The best example of this type of farm is the settlement of Swine Sty, situated high up on Big Moor, above Baslow. The land is private; it is held by the North Derbyshire Waterboard and permission to visit the site *must* be obtained from the authority. A three-sided compound of about three-quarters of an acre is bounded on the fourth side by a steep outcrop of grit. Inside the compound a circular, stone-built hut has been uncovered. Radiating from the outside of the compound are several stone walls which appear to mark the limits of fields. In this small settlement one or two families would live; grain would be grown and sheep would be grazed on the pasture above the farm. At night the animals would be brought inside the compound to protect them from the bears and wolves that still dwelt in the forest.

Soon after the Urnfolk arrived the Food Vessel people adopted cremation as their burial rite. This must have been the result of long and continued contact between the two groups of people. Just how far this mutual assimilation of cultures went is not certain for the archaeological record diminishes at this time.

5. *The Coming of the Celts*

BY 1300 B.C. Bronze Age man had started to change his natural environment but he was still unable to control it. The limestone uplands were now almost devoid of the heavy woodland that once covered the area. Fields had been cleared, abandoned to the wild vegetation and then cleared again. Much the same story had occurred on the gritstone areas. The Urnfolk had cleared fields from the oak woods but when the fertility of the soils had decreased they had abandoned their farms to the natural regeneration of the woods and had cut fresh fields. However, successive generations of farmers were altering the characteristics of the soil. Ploughing was opening up the soil to erosion and the sheep were grazing off the young saplings before they could become fully established. Inevitably, century by century, the soils above the gritstone bands became stonier, the shale soils wetter and the woodland cover poorer.

At some time between 1300 and 800 B.C. man started to move down from these uplands into the Derwent valley. Very little is known about this period, covering the Middle Bronze Age, for recorded settlements are non-existent. Speculation on abandonment of the moors stems from this lack of evidence together with the finds of the new, elaborate axes mostly in valley sites. By the Late Bronze Age, 800 - 400 B.C., we must envisage the people of Derbyshire dwelling in clearings in the valley woods. They would use the uplands as pasture for their flocks, either throughout the year or in summer only. This raises the unexplored possibility that many of the Derbyshire villages may be considerably older than has been thought previously.

The Late Bronze Age sees a marked increase in the amount and type of bronze tools available to the farmer. A bronze-smith would travel throughout a region, stopping at the isolated farms to sell his new tools or to repair those that the farmer had in his possession. Axes were now mass-produced in a two-piece mould which gave a hollowed axehead—the socketed axe. Unlike previous axes, this meant that the haft could pass inside the socket. As an additional safeguard, thongs were used to tie the haft onto the axe through a small side loop. With the change in axe morphology came a parallel change in the constituents of the metal used. From the Late Bronze Age onwards the smith began to mix lead as well as tin to his copper, thus increasing the quantity of bronze available.

Two axes of this socketed type have been found within the confines of the Mam Tor hillfort—a seemingly Iron Age settlement. Investigations of huts found here point to the use of the site from about 1100 B.C., about seven hundred years earlier than had been envisaged before. It is, of course, possible that the massive ramparts of the fort are not associated with these huts but until further work is carried out a certain amount of confusion must remain.

At the same time as the Bronze Age farmers were cultivating their fields in Derbyshire, widespread cultural changes were occurring in Continental Europe. In *circa* 1500 B.C. the technique of ironworking was mastered by the Hittites of Turkey but it was not for a further thousand years that this was to reach Britain. The collapse of the Hittite empire, *circa* 1100 B.C., allowed the secret of iron-working to escape to the peoples of Central Europe, giving rise to the Hallstatt and La Tène cultures. The Hallstatt peoples can properly be regarded as Celtic but the origins of the Celts themselves go back far into prehistory.

The arrival of iron tools and the arrival of the Celts in Britain are synonymous. By the latter half of the sixth century B.C. iron-using peoples were crossing the North Sea and settling on the coast from Wessex to Yorkshire. Despite the popular conception of the Celts as fierce warriors, they were primarily farmers and only resorted to violence when their settlements were threatened. From the coast these fair-haired people moved inland along the river valleys. There is little evidence for the arrival of the Celts in Derbyshire but this is thought to have occurred in the fifth century B.C. Pottery from a field at Brassington seems to belong to the Early Iron Age, 500-300 B.C.

The arrival of iron tools is better marked. Iron's major advantage over bronze was the wide availability of inexpensive iron ore and its suitability as a raw material for the manufacture of many different woodworking tools. It is therefore not surprising that tools were made in enormous numbers. Iron tools corrode very easily and they are rare finds on Derbyshire sites. However, their effect is recorded in the pollen

"Celtic" style stone head from Thornseats, Sheffield.

0   2   4   6
Cms.

Opposite:- Top: Iron Age group. Pottery from Back Tor (left) and near Beeston Tor (right). Saddle quern, ribbing stone and stone disc from Ball Cross, Bakewell.
Bottom: A bronze fibula from Harborough Rocks.
Above:- "Slag" from iron smelting site at Burbage Brook.

deposits in the moorland peats. Recent work has shown that there was a large increase in the clearing of the woodlands at this time. This is best explained, not by a rise in population, but by the ease with which trees could be cleared with the new axes and by the need for charcoal to help in the smelting of local ores.

The way of life of the farmers had changed little since the Early Bronze Age. Farmsteads were still isolated units, housing only one or two families. Huts were in forest clearances, made of timber and stone and with sloping roofs to combat the rainy climate. Where animal bones have been recovered from sites, they have shown that cattle, sheep, goats and pigs were kept as domesticated animals. Hunting was undertaken for two reasons. Red and roe deer were hunted for their meat and skins and animals such as the bear, wolf, fox and wild cat were removed from the local area to protect the domesticated stock. Wheat and barley were cultivated intensively. Storage pits, which are common on Iron Age sites in southern England, are absent in Derbyshire. This has been interpreted as showing that small amounts of cereals were grown, but in the uplands grain stored in pits in the ground would have soon rotted owing to heavy soil moisture. It may be that the grain was stored on covered, timber structures built high enough above the ground to protect the crop from grazing animals.

The communities were very self-sufficient. Iron was worked locally and not left to the skills of the travelling smith as had been the case in the Bronze Age. A mound of iron slag has recently been found in the Burbage Basin, near Hathersage. This was one site where iron was smelted from the ironstone nodules found in the Millstone Grit rocks. Timber, for charcoal, would have been available locally in the valley. Where the settlements are that this forge served is a mystery.

Wooden looms were used by the women to weave textiles from the wool of the sheep and goats. The looms have long since disappeared but occasionally the stone loom weights are found. Simple, functional pottery was made—none as far as we can gather specifically for funeral use. Three broad groups of pottery have been recognised. First, there are large storage jars with finger-tip decorated shoulders; second, are plain jars and bowls with flared rims and sharply rounded shoulders; third, there are rather featureless jars and bowls of a crude, undecorated fabric.

The use of iron, which was cheaper and easier to work than bronze, made the manufacture of beautiful pieces of jewellery

The Iron Age hillfort on Mam Tor. The depressions visible within this univallate fort are believed to be the foundations of huts. At the extreme crest of the ridge are two Bronze Age barrows.

possible. True Celtic artwork is uncommon in Derbyshire but in pieces such as the fine brooch from Harborough Cave there are hints of the La Tène metalwork, which swept through Britain in the first and second centuries B.C. The beautiful jewellery, elaborate swords and shields known from this period are an indication of the growing efficiency of the farmers and the increasing incomes of wealthy chiefs. With an accumulation of wealth comes the desire to accumulate more than is often possible by peaceful means. Warfare results. Sometimes it is no more vicious than the stealing of a few of a neighbour's stock but it is more likely to escalate into open feuding. In order that the weak can oppose the strong, they have to band together, forming tribes and building defensive structures. Out of this inter-tribal and inter-community warfare arose the hillforts—fortified sites used as refuges where the people and flocks from the surrounding area took shelter in times of crisis.

Seven hillforts are known in Derbyshire: Mam Tor, Ball-cross, Combs Moss, Burr Tor, Fin Cop, Castle Rings and Markland Grips. The first six named are in the Peak District; the last is on the Magnesian Limestone near Whitwell. Some forts, such as Mam Tor, have defensive ramparts which completely encircle the camp; others, such as Fin Cop, have two or three sides formed by natural cliffs and a man-made wall along one side. No visit to Castleton would be complete without a call at the Mam Tor hillfort, high up on a ridge, controlling the road through the Winnats. Two entrances lead through the ramparts into a huge plateau area pitted with the remains of prehistoric huts. The fort covers sixteen acres, and as such is the largest surviving monument of its type in Northern England. Yet it is hard to imagine that its political importance was of the same magnitude as its size. Perhaps it was only locally important. A series of fortified sites, such as these hillforts, begs the question: were they built as a unified system against a common outside enemy or were they built separately to offer the user protection against each other local fort? The answer must come from a study of the human society by which they were constructed.

Roman writers tell us that the north-east Midlands were the province of a great Celtic tribe known as the Coritani and that the Brigantes occupied the area to the north of them. Where the frontier between these two tribes was is speculative. However, the hillforts of Derbyshire were in the zone either north or south of this frontier. The pottery suggests that the Iron Age peoples of the Peak formed a tribe that was allied to the loose federation of predominantly Bronze Age tribes called the Brigantes. But southern Derbyshire lay in the lands of the Coritani. These hillforts therefore may have been built by a Brigantian tribe as a protection against the Coritani raiders from the south. Whatever their original purpose, when the brief rule of the Celts was brought to an end by the Romans the forts would undoubtedly have been turned into refuges against this new, powerful enemy.

6. *Under Roman Influences*

IN A.D. 43 Aulus Plautius brought southern Britain into the Roman Empire but it was another five years before Roman troops were seen in Derbyshire. The second Governor of Britain, Ostorius Scapula, had conquered the Coritani of the Midlands by A.D. 48 and had established a temporary frontier along the Trent. Now his choice lay between a campaign against the British in the Welsh hills or an attack upon the far-flung Brigantes, stretched from the Irish Sea to the North Sea and from the Trent to the Tweed. He seems to have reached an agreement with the Brigantian queen, Cartimandua, before successfully attempting to crush the resistance in Wales. Peace in Derbyshire was short-lived for the Roman troops crossed the Trent *circa* A.D. 50 and built a fort on the west bank of the Derwent, in what is now Strutt's Park, Derby. This site was opposite the later fort of Derbentione, or Little Chester. They then moved forward to the Don and established a fort at Templeborough, Sheffield.

In spite of these incursions Derbyshire was largely free from Roman influences until the Governorship of Agricola began in A.D. 78. Agricola had forts built at Brough, Buxton, Melandra near Glossop, Pentrich and possibly Chesterfield, and rather surprisingly the fort at Strutt's Park was abandoned in favour of a new fort at Little Chester on the lower east bank of the Derwent. Roads were constructed to link these forts, thus helping to coerce the inhabitants of the area into a peaceful mode of life and facilitating the general communications of the British province.

After the conquest of Brigantia the Romans were not prepared just to police the area; the natives had to pay for the *Pax Romana*. The Roman Empire was eager to receive many of the goods that Britain could produce. Derbyshire's contribution to the British exports was to be lead ore, found as galena in large veins within the Carboniferous Limestone formation. The Romans quickly discovered and exploited the lead deposits for, although the only datable material of this industry comes from the reign of Hadrian, A.D. 117-138, it is likely that Roman miners were busy in Derbyshire at least thirty years earlier, *circa* A.D. 80.

Mining was centred in the south-east of the limestone plateau in the Wirksworth-Matlock area, where three probable mines have been found. Pigs of lead from this region often bear the abbreviation LVT, believed to be a contraction for *Lutudaron* which appears to have been the fort/town in which the lead processing was done. The location of Lutudaron has been lost in antiquity, although sites at Wirksworth, Matlock, Rainster Rocks and Chesterfield have been put forward as claimants to the name. The lead field was developed by the Imperial government at the time of Hadrian, but at some period a private company, the *socii Lutudarenses*, held the concession. Lead pigs bearing their mark have been found at

A pig of lead found near Matlock Bath in 1783. The inscription reads, when translated: Lucius Aruconius Verecundus, from the mines of Lutudaron.

Petuaria (Brough on Humber, Yorkshire) from where they were probably exported.

Lead was not only mined, it was also extracted from the stream deposits near the fort at Brough, Derbyshire. This implies that there was a well-developed system of collection by the native population for whom the fort served as a central depot. Convict labour and slaves were often used in Roman mines as a form of penal servitude. There is a tradition around Brough that the Bradwell people thought of the Castleton folk as being descended from slaves, though the Castleton folk retorted that the Bradwell people were descended from convicts. Perhaps in this piece of folk-lore we have some evidence for the first Derbyshire lead miners, though the point should not be pressed.

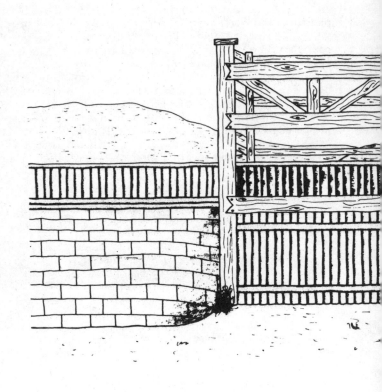

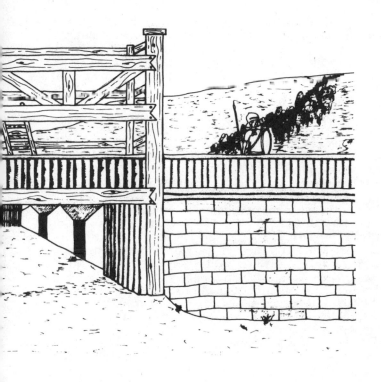

A possible reconstruction of one of the entrances to the fort at Brough (Navio), taken from the rebuilt Roman fort at the Lunt, Coventry.

It is unnecessary to give a detailed history of all the Roman forts as many events that occurred in their history are common to all. Brough, in the north of the county, is taken as a rather simplified example. The Roman name of the station was either *Navio* or *Anavio*. Agricola had Brough constructed in A.D. 78-79 on land in the angle formed by the confluence of the river Noe and Bradwell Brook. Protection from a surprise attack was therefore guaranteed on these two sides and its position gave the Romans military dominance over the upper Derwent valley. They used the fort not only as a military station but also as a collecting centre for the local lead industry.

About A.D.140 the fort was abandoned, together with the others in Derbyshire, to provide Lollius Urbicus with enough troops for his campaigns in Scotland. Presumably he thought that the Celtic tribes of Northern England were now peaceful. Any such assumption was proved wrong in A.D.155-158 when the Brigantian tribes took the opportunity to break into open revolt. Reinforcements had to be drafted in from the German provinces to suppress the rebellion. The result of this uprising was that Brough was rebuilt, as an inscription shows us, in A.D.158 by the First Cohort of Aquitanians, who stayed on as its garrison. The fort was small by Roman standards being about 90 yards by 110 yards, with a gateway at the centre of each wall. Wooden barracks inside the walls housed the five hundred strong garrison but buildings such as the bathhouse were built outside the fort. Brough has yielded artifacts of many types: swords, coins, bridle bits, spears, tiles, native pottery, Roman Samian ware, lead fragments, catapult balls, and reputedly a rough bust of Apollo. The fort seems to have been abandoned again about A.D.220 but was reinstated for police and fiscal activities *circa* A.D.260, probably as a result of local disturbances. The occupation at Brough ceased about A.D.360.

Whether or not the Roman troops mixed socially with the Celts is difficult to answer. Evidence for the troop's presence at Brough is not limited to the site of the fort. At Haddon, near Bakewell, a Roman altar was found inscribed "To the God *Mars Braciaca,* erected by J. Sittius Caeciliamus, praefect of the First Cohort of Aquitaine", who it will be remembered was the garrison at Brough. The altar is now on display at Haddon Hall.

It was not uncommon for a classical god, such as Mars, to become associated with the name of a native deity, in this case Braciaca. We know little of this native god but as the basis of Celtic religion was animism it is likely to refer to a spirit of the

The Roman road from Buxton to Brough. It continues across the left centre of the photograph to the fort at Brough, near the artificial lakes at the extreme left.

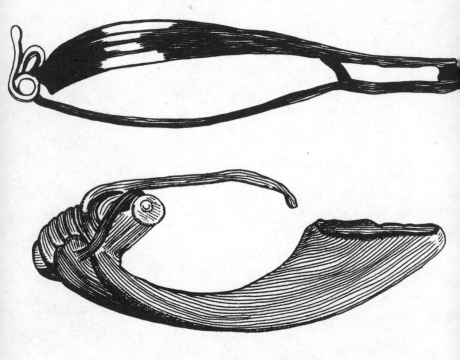

Top: Bronze fibula found at Ringham Low, Monyash.
Bottom: Bronze harp-shaped fibula found on excavating for a mill pond at Middleton-by-Youlgreave.

hills, woods or streams, He—presumably he was a male since the name was linked with that of Mars—was only one of the endless throng of deities that were worshipped in Derbyshire but all were subservient to the mother goddess *Brigantia*. This goddess of water was promoted by the Romans to the status of Jupiter on good political grounds. The well-dressing ceremonies of northern Derbyshire, now associated with Christian beliefs, may extend back to the worshipping of Brigantia.

Another Celtic goddess, *Arnemetia,* gave her name to the civilian settlement established by the Romans at Buxton. *Aquae Arnemetiae,* as the town became known, may have started as an Iron Age village or temple in a grove sacred to Arnemetia. The naturally warm mineral springs in the vicinity of Buxton were recognised by the Romans, who established a fort there at the time of Agricola. The usefulness of the fort must have diminished and it was abandoned to be replaced by a civilian settlement. Buxton became a spa town, second in importance only to Bath. Lead-lined baths associated with Roman remains at St. Anne's Wells were found in the seventeenth century.

The arrival of the Roman troops did not destroy the native economy. Far from it, as the Celtic farmers appear to have expanded not only the area under cultivation but also the number of crops grown. The economic base for the majority of the population was still provided by agriculture, but the emphasis was slowly changing from pastoralism to mixed-farming. The need to provide food for the Roman soldiers garrisoning the forts might have been the stimulus to grow increasing amounts of grain. Pollen records reveal that still further amounts of woodland were cleared, probably to cope with the increase in arable cultivation. New crops, such as rye, walnut and hops, were brought by the Romans from the Continent and were assimilated into the farming systems of the Celts.

On the limestone uplands many native farmsteads have been recognised but apart from surface surveying little explorative work has been done on them. These farmsteads are concentrated in two areas: one stretches along the top of the Wye gorge from Buxton, the second is in the Castleton area near Brough. At Chee Tor, Blackwell, on a promontory overlooking the river Wye, F. Thomas found and examined a series of low banks which proved to mark the foundations of a native settlement. There are some "Celtic" fields to the south-east, which are almost certainly associated with this settlement. No artifacts are known from the site. With most of the known farmsteads being concentratèd on the margins of the limestone plateau one begins to wonder whether or not the centre of the plateau might also have been fully farmed. It could be that later activity has destroyed the evidence.

A Romano-British site was also uncovered at Owslow Farm, Carsington. From the site, on gently sloping land sheltered from the north, comes a pig of lead and some Derbyshire Ware pottery dated to the second or third century A.D. It is probable, as has been the case throughout Derbyshire prehistory, that this was an isolated farmstead largely self-sufficient in agricultural products.

From the Neolithic Period onwards the Magnesian Limestone ridge was apparently shunned by man, but in the Roman Period he seems to have chosen, or been forced, to settle along this belt. There is evidence from Anston and near Killamarsh in Yorkshire, from Whitwell, Langwith, Shirebrook and Pleasley in Derbyshire and from Mansfield Woodhouse in Nottinghamshire for this "take-over" of the Magnesian Limestone. The best excavated example of a native farmstead is just over the north-eastern border in Yorkshire—at Scratta Wood. Poetic licence for this non-Derbyshire example is sought from the reader on the grounds that there was no county boundary in Roman times! The enclosure, which had an oval perimeter wall with internal sub-divisions and the remains of huts, has yielded Roman pottery and fibulae (brooches of safety-pin form) belonging to the second and third centuries A.D. Sherds of a crude, dark native ware have been thought to extend back into the Iron Age but this is far from certain.

Bronze finds and coins from these sites are rare and the conclusion drawn is that the Magnesian Limestone had a reasonably large population which appears to have been far from affluent. The people lived in a series of isolated farmsteads growing cereals, keeping domestic cattle and sheep and hunting deer. The pottery so far discovered was made mostly at the Cantley potteries near Templeborough, Yorkshire, and Derbyshire Ware is poorly represented. These settlements must, therefore, have been on the edge of the area served by the Derbyshire Ware kilns.

The mining and smelting of lead was not the only important industrial activity. Pottery-making had developed from a family chore, through a localised industry to what may be regarded as a considerable manufacturing industry. Although there was a large number of types of pots, many were only produced in limited amounts. One style, however, was "mass-

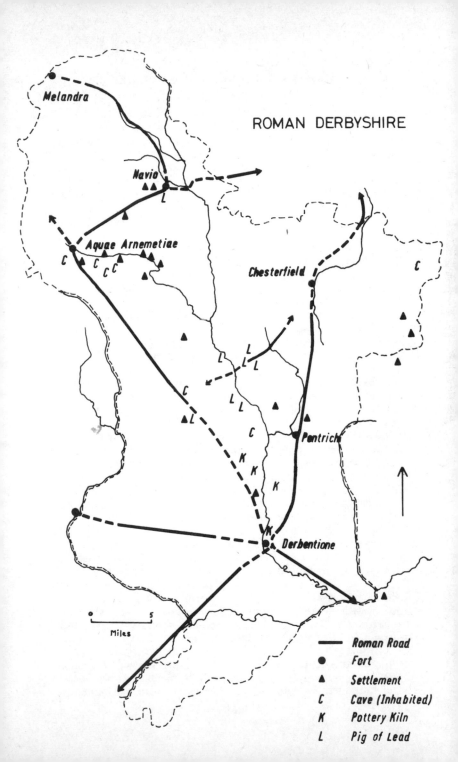

ROMAN DERBYSHIRE

Melandra

Navio

Aquae Arnemetiae

Chesterfield

Pentrich

Derbentione

Miles

——— Roman Road
● Fort
▲ Settlement
C Cave (Inhabited)
K Pottery Kiln
L Pig of Lead

produced" and exported throughout Northern England. This pottery, which was made for approximately two hundred years, is known as Derbyshire Ware. Recent excavations have unearthed some of the kilns used in its manufacture and have made it possible to produce a brief history of this industry.

Four kilns have been excavated—Hazelwood, Holbrook, Shottle Hall and Little Chester. The earliest site is at Little Chester where the kilns were in operation during the Trajanic period (A.D.98-117). The clay used in the pottery-making process appears to come from some distance away at Chaddesden and Borrowash. A great variety of pottery was made, including an early form of Derbyshire Ware. Production of the pottery was then either switched to Holbrook or this second pottery was opened to meet increased demand. Holbrook was in use in the late second century and may have been the source of Derbyshire Ware found in the Antoinine levels of the forts of the county. Local clay was used in these kilns. The Shottle Hall kilns came into use shortly after this with production later being increased by a further pottery at Hazelwood, where there is an abundant local supply of fuel, water and clay.

Derbyshire Ware is found throughout Northern England, as far north as Hadrian's Wall. The internal distribution within the county shows that, although the kilns were between Wirksworth and Derby, much of the Derbyshire Ware is found on the northern hills. This is not surprising for the northern areas are those where the agricultural economy would make some imports necessary. There seems to be a clear link between the pottery finds and the known Roman and prehistoric roads. Indeed Hopton, Hazelwood and Shottle Hall are all situated on or near the Old Portway, which is a prehistoric track running from Nottingham north-westwards to somewhere in the vicinity of Mam Tor.

The pottery was used as storage jars, and the suggestion has been put forward that these were made to carry supplies of beans which were probably grown in the Trent valley. The Romans, of course, had their own wide variety of bowls, dishes, jars, jugs, etc. "Samian" Ware, which is a hard, red pottery with molded designs, is known from the sites of the Roman forts. This ware was imported from southern and central Gaul in the first three centuries A.D., but was occasionally made in England, for example, at Colchester, Essex.

One curious feature of native Derbyshire life was the continued use of caves as living-quarters. Sufficient of these have been examined to show that the caves were permanently occupied, and not used merely as hideouts or shelters. The reason for this is not hard to find; a cave offers a ready-made and warm, if occasionally wet, shelter from the elements. At Hartle Dale Caves, Bradwell, a bronze coin of Valens (A.D.364-378), fragments of a coarse ware of the third century and some coloured coated ware have been discovered. Many other caves from the Carboniferous Limestone plateau, such as Thirst House and Pooles Cavern at Carlswark, have yielded Samian and Derbyshire Ware, Roman coins and Bronze fibulae. Robin Hood's Cave at Creswell makes a re-appearance in the records with finds of Romano-British antiquities.

The Romans did not introduce coinage into Derbyshire, but recorded finds of coins previous to the arrival of the troops are rare. A hoard of Cortani coins has been found at Ashford-in-the-Water. This is thought to represent nothing more than the flight of Cortani refugees into Brigantian territory in front of the advancing Romans. Some of the commonest small finds of this period are the Roman coins. Bateman often found them when excavating the Derbyshire barrows; they are common on all Roman sites and have sometimes turned up buried in urns. In 1748 an urn was unearthed near Alfreton which contained sixteen hundred Roman denarii. Coin finds at Chesterfield add to the argument for a fort in this town. Coins have also been found on the gritstone moorlands above Hathersage, even though the soil conditions are alien to the preservation of bronze.

Much of the Bronze Age story was taken up with a discussion of different burial rituals. Dead Romans also had to be buried. Before the Edict of Milan of A.D.313 officially made Christianity acceptable to the Roman Empire, some Romans were buried in the previously used barrows. A small bronze coin of Constantius Chlorus, a knife, a comb and a few fragments of Romano-British pottery attest to the use of Rusden Low for a Roman interment. After the introduction of Christianity, the use of barrows became regarded as a pagan habit and was replaced by a normal grave.

Events in Roman Britain were often dependent upon events in Rome. When Rome was threatened by the massed armies of "barbarians" from North and East Europe, the Roman garrisons were withdrawn from Britain. These "barbarians", in the form of Scots, Picts, Angles and Saxons, were also threatening the peace of Britain. In A.D.410 Honorius, the western Emperor, authorised the Britons to look to their own defences. It was hoped that this was only a temporary expedient until Britain could be returned to the Empire. The hope was to go unfilled—the "barbarians" invaded from the west, north and east and stayed.

7. *Anglian and Danish Settlers*

IN an attempt to hold back the marauding Picts and Scots, Vortigern, the overall British commander, encouraged the Angles and Saxons to come to Britain as mercenary soldiers. For this act, which many of his contemporaries would have regarded as the correct course of action, Vortigern has been branded as the man who lost Britain to the Saxons. In fact the blame cannot be attached to any one man. With the central authority of the Romans gone, the British began to collapse back into local tribes. As the Angles and Saxons increased in numbers they could use this weak British situation for their own benefit. The Saxon rebellion in the mid-fifth century A.D. resulted in the formation of their own kingdoms, such as Deira in Yorkshire and another in Kent. The British, under the leadership of Ambrosius Aurelianus and then Arthur, rallied to meet the threat. Arthur—never a "King", only a cavalry commander—fought the decisive battle at *Mons Badonicus*. Won by the Britons, it not only established peace for the next fifty years but also led to large numbers of Anglo-Saxons returning to their homelands.

In this "Dark Age" period, Derbyshire appears to have been untroubled by these events. Probably the Angles had never penetrated to the county before they were defeated by Arthur. Of the surviving British population we know little. Undoubtedly some of the men would have joined the British armies in the south but the remainder would have carried on their normal farming life.

Peace with the German peoples did not last, the kingdom of Deira still remaining as a focal point for Anglian resistance. About A.D.550 the Angles, supplemented by large numbers from the Continent, began to settle along the Trent valley. From a study of place-names here and from the archaeological evidence we can see that the earliest Anglian settlements were in the valley below Nottingham. One ancient place-name in Derbyshire—Repton, which means "hill of the *Hrype*"—is a record of an early settlement established by people from the same tribe as those that settled at Ripon in North Yorkshire.

To the south of these settlements were the friendly kingdoms of the Saxons but to the north were the unconquered Britons. The British in the west of Yorkshire responded to the Anglian challenge by coming together as the kingdom of Elmet, a stronghold which was not conquered by the English until the early seventh century. In Derbyshire it has been suggested by the Rev. J. H. Brooksbank that the Britons of north Derbyshire, led by a British king called Gwyn, similarly held out as the kingdom of Orcoit, with a great fortress on Win Hill serving as the capital. Remains of the fort have never been found but there is every indication that Anglian settlement did not take place in this upland region until into the seventh century.

Expansion of the Anglian groups throughout the Midlands led to the foundation of many new settlements. The Anglian kingdom of Mercia (derived from *Mierce* meaning the "borderers") encompassed Derbyshire and the rest of the Midlands. Mercian settlements were established deep in the heart of the Derwent valley at places such as Rowsley, Beeley, Wensley, Lea, Darley, Padley, Pilsley, etc. The common feature of these names is the element *leah*, meaning "wood" or "open land", sufficient indication that the floor of the valley was still well-wooded. The limestone uplands and the Keuper Marl Lowlands were also settled at this time.

The Britons cannot have relinquished their lands without a struggle, and two monuments attest to the fighting that must have occurred. To the east of Hathersage is the undated fort known as Carl Wark. The form of its defences in no way suggests the Iron Age date attributed to the other Derbyshire hillforts. However, at the west end of the fort is a monumentous stone wall backed by a turf rampart. A "Dark Age" date for this type of construction has been put forward by C. Piggott. Can this fort be the last bastion of British resistance against the Mercian invaders?

Four or five miles to the west of this fort is an earthwork known as Grey Ditch. It is a longitudinal bank and ditch cutting the line of the Roman road in Bradwell Dale and limiting entry on to the limestone uplands by enemies from the north. Some historians have seen the earthwork as an attempt by isolated British communities to prevent Angles from the Hope valley gaining admittance to the limestone plateau. It is more likely that the reverse is true; that is, that the earthwork was built by Mercians who had entered the limestone region from the south and were anxious to protect themselves from the Britons in the north Derwent valley.

By A.D. 650, when the heathen Mercian king, Penda, ruled

Carl Wark, a British fort above Hathersage.

Derbyshire, there were some 1200 families of the Pec Saetas (Peak-dwellers) of which 700 were in Derbyshire and 500 in Cheshire.

For further understanding of the history of the settlement of Derbyshire it is necessary to emphasise one often forgotten fact. It was the Britons who were Christians and the Angles who were pagans. This situation was to alter. On the eve of Easter Day 627 the Northumbrian king, Edwin, was baptised into the Christian faith by Paulinus. Edwin invaded the British kingdom of Gwynedd in North Wales forcing Cad-wallon, king of Gwynedd, to turn to the heathen Penda for help. Hoping to destory the Christian faith and establish Mercia as the ruling royal house of northern England, Penda and Cadwallon's forces invaded Northumbria, defeating Edwin's army and killing Edwin at an unknown site in Hatfield Chase near Doncaster. For the next twenty years bitter power struggles between the two Anglian royal families were carried on, with first one side then the other gaining the upper hand. When Penda was killed in 654 he was still a heathen but a year earlier one of his sons, Peada, had become a Christian on the occasion of his marriage into the Northumbrian royal family. On returning to the Mercian palace at Repton, Peada brought with him four monks—Adda, Betti, Chedd and Diuma. A bishopric was subsequently established among the Mercians with Diuma as the first bishop.

In Wirksworth church there is a carved stone slab which was found covering a skeleton near the altar. The carved figures on the top represent scenes in the life of Christ. It is widely accepted that this coffin lid covered the body of Betti, one of the four monks, after he died about A.D. 692. This in turn suggests that Wirksworth was already a town of some importance with a church, which was an offshoot of the cathedral at Repton.

Changing religious attitudes also manifested themselves in the burial rituals of the Angles. Pre-Christian burials differed through time and in area. The earliest Anglian burials were in the Trent valley, and were flat cremations in elaborate urns, but by the time that the uplands of Derbyshire had been settled, poorly furnished inhumation cemeteries and barrow burials had come into fashion. The only two early cemeteries in the uplands are at Overton Hall and Curbar, where five burials have been recorded.

The return to the use of pagan barrow burials is interesting. Not only were burials inserted in existing barrows, but new barrows were constructed which have yielded some very

The Anglian Benty Grange helmet.

Above: A leather drinking cup found with the Benty Grange burial.
Opposite: Gold Cross from Winster Moor.

exciting finds. As before it was Thomas Bateman who did many of the excavations. At Brushfield, overlooking Cressbrook Dale, he opened a "fairly shaped barrow" to find a human body resting on a skin and coffin base. This Anglian warrior had been buried with a "long and broad iron sword, enclosed in a sheath made of thin wood covered with ornamental leather." Under the hilt was a short iron knife and nearby were the remains of two javelin heads and a shield. Probably the most important find of Bateman's career came from a barrow at Benty Grange Farm, south of Buxton on the Ashbourne road. The burial is again an Anglian warrior—one of noble birth to judge from the artifacts. A large mass of oxidised iron near the rotted remains of the skeleton turned out to be a coat of chainwork and a frame of a helmet.

The Benty Grange helmet is now justly famous throughout Europe. It consists of a skeleton formed of iron bands, radiating from the crown of the head and riveted to a circle of iron which encompassed the brow. Attached to the iron straps are two figures whose presence seems to contradict each other. One is a small silver cross, slightly ornamented round the edges, with its deeply Christian connotations. The second figure is that of a hog, fastened to the crown of the helmet. The hog was sacred to the god Freyr, which implies the warrior was a pagan. There are other cases of articles bearing crosses being found in Anglian barrows. Perhaps these burials were made when the changeover from the old gods to Christianity was taking place. A leather drinking cup was also found in the Benty Grange excavation. It was three inches high, with a silver rim, four circular ornaments and two silver crosses (again!) as decorations.

Anglian finds from barrows include: beads of amber, amethyst and glass, brooches of gold or copper, enriched with garnets and coloured glass, pins of gold and bronze, silver needles, small bronze boxes, iron knives, swords, spears and coats of chain. A simple catalogue may convey the immense variety of artifacts, but it cannot demonstrate the beauty of pieces of jewellery such as the Winster Cross. Discovered in a barrow on Winster Moor in 1776, this cross of pure gold has a cut garnet set in its centre and is ornamented with delicate filigree work. The whole piece is only $1\frac{1}{2}$ inches long, A visit to Sheffield City Museum where the cross is on show is worthwhile just to see this one object. This burial must belong to a Christian, but whether the deceased was an Angle or a Briton is difficult to establish.

After the adoption of Christianity we lose the distinctive

burials of the past. A grave from the seventh century is little different from that of the fourteenth century or even the twentieth century. Religion was just one facet of the life of the people. The Anglian community was essentially a rural one, where the economy was based on agriculture. Nevertheless the elaborate pieces of jewellery found show that the community could support craftsmen turning out expensive work.

On to the patchwork of British farms, fields and woodlands the newcomers introduced a new economic system which has largely shaped the Derbyshire countryside that we know today. The most significant introduction was the rural village. Towns had been in use in Roman Derbyshire but the majority of the population lived in single farmsteads. The adoption of village life may have stemmed from differences between the Anglian and British society which are not yet understood.

A typical Anglian settlement conjures up the picture of a

An Anglo-Saxon plough depicted on the Bayeux Tapestry.

fairly large number of small rectangular huts surrounded by the fields. As the society was hierarchical some of the villages must have had a hall in which lived the nobleman who controlled the surrounding agricultural settlements. From this arrangement the manorial system developed. Even as late as the Domesday census certain villages of Derbyshire were "linked" with the entries of a main village; e.g. Hope, which has seven linked entries of Edale, Aston, Shatton, Offerton, Tideswell, Stoke and *Munchedesuuelle*.

The Anglians used a heavy plough drawn by a number of oxen, enabling them to plough the heavier soils of the valley floors and use the clay soils of the Keuper Marl Lowlands. Settlement in this latter area must date from this period. Evidence of Anglian farming techniques is rather limited in Derbyshire but from elsewhere in Britain we know that the common cereals were barley, wheat and oats, with some flax for cloth-making. Grain was milled locally, perhaps using water power from the Southern Pennine streams.

The pastoral side of Anglian agriculture was still based on the breeding of cattle, sheep, goats and pigs. Perhaps there was a tendency to increase the number of cattle kept at the expense of sheep, although this number was limited by the amount of grain available for fodder throughout the winter. After fattening during the summer months the least promising beasts would be slaughtered in autumn, the meat being salted to preserve it for winter consumption. Only the strongest cattle were kept alive through the winter and these would be so weak through the lack of fodder that they would have to be carried into the fields when spring arrived. The increased clearance of the valley woodlands is reflected in the pollen record of East Moor. On the gritstone uplands the soil had deteriorated to such an extent that it almost precluded tree growth, leaving the area fit for little but sheep grazing.

Lead mining had been carried on by the Britons after the Romans withdrew, and the lead-fields fell into Anglian hands and were worked by them. We know that in 835 Wirksworth was granted to Duke Humbert in return for an annual grant of lead to Canterbury cathedral.

Divorced as they were from the centre of the political struggles of the Anglo-Saxon royal houses, these rural communities cannot have been unaffected by them. In 757 Aethelbald, king of the Mercians, was slain at Sockington and his body buried at Repton. By the 820s Wessex was on the upsurge and the Mercians were overthrown by Egbert, who advanced as far as the southern border at Dore near Sheffield where the Northumbrians offered him their submission. Egbert now ruled all England but profound political changes were in the offing, not from within the Anglo-Saxons but from invaders from the Continent. The Vikings and Danes had arrived.

A great army of Scandinavians landed in East Anglia in the autumn of 865 and in the next five years they destroyed the ancient kingdoms of Northumbria, East Anglia and Mercia. The Danes held control of the five boroughs of the east Midlands—Nottingham, Leicester, Lincoln, Stamford and Derby. In 874 the Danish army moved from Lindsay to Repton and took up winter quarters there. A Viking axe found at Repton is some indication of this occupation. This time the army left Derbyshire but between 876-880 the Danes settled in force on the lands they had conquered. A portion of the Danish army was settled at Derby to control the area that ultimately became recognised as the county of Derbyshire. The site of Derby shows many of the stages that settlements in Derbyshire passed through. Apparently founded by the Romans, a small Romano-British community grew up around the fort. The Anglians used the same site for their village called *Northworthig*, but with the Danish settlement a new town of Derby was founded which eventually grew to take over the sites of its predecessors.

At Ingleby, south of the Trent, there is a Danish pagan cemetery. Sixty or seventy burial mounds are known, some of which have yielded metalwork and in one case a Danish sword. There is little doubt that this site shows the archaeological traces of the very first phase of Danish settlement in England.

Although most of the place-names of the county are derived from Anglian sources, Danish settlement is shown by certain Old Scandinavian terms making up some place-names. A frequently quoted example is where *-by* makes up a portion of a name, as in Derby or Ingleby. But names such as Rowland, Holme and Flagg are also of Danish origin. The shortage of Danish names in north Derbyshire should not be taken as demonstrating a lack of Danish influence in that area. A charter of 926 shows that King Athelstan bought land at Ashford and Hope from "a heathen" (a Dane) to give to one of his subjects. In this upland region the Danes may have been prepared to act as overlords to the Anglian community.

In 917 Aethelflaed, lady of the Mercians, succeeded in recapturing "the borough which is called Derby, with all that belongs it" from the Danes. King Edward marched his army through the Peak District and ordered a fortress to be built and manned at Bakewell. The political boundaries between Anglian and Dane were never fully established and the Danes reoccupied Derby before it was again recaptured in 942 for the Anglians.

Some Danes had become Christians and their influence is felt in a few of the stone crosses found throughout the county. The carving and displaying of these was practised by the Anglians before the Danes invaded. The Eyam Cross, standing in the churchyard, is a beautiful example of eighth century Anglian work. It is 8 feet 3 inches high, although the upper part of the shaft is missing. There are many other crosses still remaining, too many to name, but they include those at Ashbourne, Brailsford, Baslow, Bakewell, Eyam, Hope, Norbury and Great Longstone. From 700-850 a time of Mercian prosperity led to the production of crosses of purely

The eighth century Anglian cross in Eyam churchyard. The top stone of the shaft is missing.

Anglian design. This is followed by a break in the sequence which is equated with the pagan Danish period. Memorial crosses surviving from the following period, 900-1050, clearly show the influence of Scandinavian hands, though not to the exclusion of Anglian technique.

The association of Scandinavian and Anglian influences demonstrated in the later crosses is only a reflection of the intermingling of the two nations on a broader scale. All the factions of society—Dane, Viking, Anglian, Saxon, Celt and Norseman—were to become fused into the "English" nation that was to try to resist the new threat from Normandy. By the arrival of the Normans the pattern of rural settlement in Derbyshire was very nearly complete. The Domesday Book shows us that from the end of the eleventh century to the present-day there has been little significant change in this pattern.

Man had come a long way from the time that his ancestors had sheltered in caves at Creswell. The Ice Ages had come and gone; farming had been introduced; metals were used for man's benefit; Mediterranean influences had arrived and departed with the Romans; the gritstone uplands had been deforested, settled and abandoned; the Angles had conquered the heavy clay soils of southern Derbyshire but had not been able to conquer the Scandinavians; and villages had been established that were to survive the industrial changes of the next thousand years.

Reference Section

Gazetteer of Sites

The most useful maps of Derbyshire are the 1″ O.S. sheets 111 and 120, or the 1″ O.S. Peak District Tourist Map. All sites are in the SK 100 metres grid.

Palaeolithic and Mesolithic

Creswell Crags	5374

Neolithic and Beaker

Arbor Low	162636
Bole Hill	183677
Bull Ring	078782
Five Wells	124710
Green Low	232581
Harborough	242552
Minninglow	209573
Ringham Low	169664
Stoney Low	213582
Swarkeston	376295
Willington	288278

Bronze and Iron Age

Ballcross	228691
Burr Tor	180783
Castle Rings	221629
Combs Moss	054785
Fin Cop	175710
Froggatt Edge	255764
Mam Tor	128838
Stanton Moor	2463
Swine Sty	272750

Roman

Brough	182827
Chee Tor	125734
Hazelwood	327469
Holbrook	363446
Little Chester	353375
Melandra	009951

Owslow Farm   236529
Pentrich   385541
Shottle Hall   314475

Anglian
Benty Grange   146643
Carl Wark (British)   260814
Grey Ditch   176815
Ingleby   343260
Repton   300270

Acknowledgements

The following photographs appear by permission of Sheffield City Museums:

Page 31
Page 40
Page 46
Page 57
Page 58 (top)
Page 81
Page 83

J. K. St. Joseph has supplied the following photographs from the Cambridge University Collection (Copyright reserved):

Page 39
Page 61

The Trustees of the British Museum have given permission for the use of the following photographs:

Page 58 (bottom)
Page 65

All uncredited photographs are taken by the author.
The sketches and some of the diagrams are by my wife, Maxine Whitaker. The remaining diagrams are by the author.